ESSENTIAL HUMANITY:

A Conceptual Clarity

BY

J.J. BHATT

1

ISBN:

9798830377164

Title:

Essential Humanity: *A Conceptual Clarity*

Author:

J.J. Bhatt

Published and Distributed by Amazon and Kindle worldwide.

This book is manufactured in the Unites States of America.

Books by J.J. Bhatt

HUMAN ENDEAVOR: *Essence & Mission,* (2011).

ROLLING SPIRITS: *Being Becoming* /A Trilogy, (2012)

ODYSSEY OF THE DAMNED: *A Revolving Destiny,* (2013).

PARISHRAM: *Journey of the Human Spirits,* (2014).

TRIUMPH OF THE BOLD: *A Poetic Reality,* (2015).

THEATER OF WISDOM, *(2016).*

MAGNIFICENT QUEST: *Life, Death & Eternity,* (2016).

ESSENCE OF INDIA: *A Comprehensive Perspective,* (2016).

ESSENCE OF CHINA: *Challenges & Possibilities,* (2016).

BEING & MORAL PERSUASION: *A Bolt of Inspiration,* (2017).

REFELCTIONS, RECOLLECTIONS & EXPRESSIONS, (2018).

ONE, TWO, THREE... ETERNITY: *A Poetic Odyssey, (*2018).

INDIA: *Journey of Enlightenment,* (2019a).

SPINNING MIND, SPINNING TIME: *C'est la vie,* (2019b).Book 1.

MEDITATION ON HOLY TRINITY, *(2019c), Book 2.*

ENLIGHTENMENT: *Fiat lux,* (2019d), Book 3.

BEING IN THE CONTEXTUAL ORBIT, (2019e).

QUINTESSENCE: *Thought & Action,* (2019f).

THE WILL TO ASCENT: *Power of Boldness & Genius,* (2019g).

RIDE ON A SPINNING WHEEL: *Existence Introspected, (*2020a).

A FLASH OF LIGHT: *Splendors, Perplexities & Riddles,* (2020b).

ON A ZIG ZAG TRAIL: *The Flow of Life*, (2020c).

UNBOUNDED: *An Inner Sense of Destiny* (2020d).

REVERBERATIONS: The *Cosmic Pulse,* (2020e).

LIGHT & DARK: *Dialogue and Meaning,* (2021a).

ROLLING REALITY: *Being in flux, (2021b).*

FORMAL SPLENDOR: *The Inner Rigor,* (2021c).

TEMPORAL TO ETERNAL: *Unknown Expedition,* (2021d).

TRAILBLAZERS: *Spears of Courage,* (2021e).

TRIALS & ERRORS: *A Path to Human Understanding*, (2021f).

MEASURE OF HUMAN EXPERIENCE: *Brief Notes,* (2021g).

LIFE: *An Ellipsis (2022a).*

VALIDATION: *The Inner Realm of Essence* (2022b).

LET'S ROLL: *Brave Heart,* (2022c).

BEING BECOMING, (2022d).

Also: INVINCIBLE, (2022e); THE CODE: *DESTINY* (2022f);

LIFE DIMYSTIFIED, (2022g); SPIRALING SPHERES (2022h).

ESSENTIAL HUMANITY: *A Conceptual Clarity* (2022i);

DISCOURSE: *Being & Meaning* (2022j).

Preface

ESSENTIAL HUMANITY: *A Conceptual Clarity* requires how modern humans be liberated from the prevailing hedonistic and techno-oriented life style and restore to their genuine identity what is humanity. The Essence of humanity seems, "What is a basic human to be at the core."

In the final analysis, it is in understanding the moral nature of humanity that holds a harmonious and hopeful future for the generations to follow. Today is the time to prepare for and act upon the right blueprint for tomorrow. In turn, for our timely and collective endeavor; children may well say, "Thank you all for looking after us."

J.J. Bhatt

Contents

7

Endless

Well read
Books of wisdom,
Many in numbers

Still
Not enough
To know,
"What is it all
About?"

Listened
Many great
Minds and
There is no
Full progress to
Report

Million
Reasons
Came and gone
While along the
Track and still lost

Well, that's
The story of
Humanity in
Quest of its
Truth...

Be Bold

When
Caught by
The vagaries of
The troubled time
Let there be light

When
Trapped into a
Stygian night,
Let the illumined
Soul show us
The real path

And,
Let there
Be clarity to
Make-it all
The way to meet
The Moral Self...

Closure

Don't you
Dare exclude
Metaphysical
Reality
For you can't

Don't
Drop the cause
That you can't
Grasp through
The conceptual
Mind

Don't dismiss
The things or
Events that you
Can't conceive
In your time

There is
Ever present,
World beyond

That is
Where your
Truth waits, if you
Know the value of
Your humanity with
Calm and alert...

Our
Time

Why have
We forgotten
To breathe fresh air,
Drink good water and
Have a quality diet

Why it is
Not happening
In our time and

Why let our
Natural rights
Be hijacked by
The greed driven
Big boys

No wonder,
These cheap junk
Foods, bad air and
Unhealthy waters;
Making millions fat,
Sick and throwing 'em
To the painful deaths...

Journey

This
Ignorance,
What a bleeding
Curse;
Hiding the beauty
And truth always

This
Pseudo-arrogance,
What a sustained
State of anxiety
And fear

This
Indifferent attitude
What a tacit cause of
Bigotry, blood-spills
And even deaths

So long,
The trio rules;
No prospect for
Peace, progress and
Prosperity to be the
Genuine experience,
Being human...

Action,
Please

So we've
Been talking so
Loudly of freedom,
Justice and equality
Yet, why do we
End up so short?

Seems,
All looks so good
In words and on the
Gold pages, but
There is always
Half- and half action
In return

Is it the
Education at fault,
Is it the arrogance?
Or is it the
Sheer ignorance;
Not ready to lift the
Quasi-animals to the
Top!

Rethink

Great
Thinkers
Probed different
Dimensions within
Their conceptual
Reference

Many great
Minds asked
"To know the
Moral Self, well"

Sadly, the
Noble Goals still
Not in the hand and

That's been
The *leit motif*
Since inception
That's been
The failed base
Reference thus far...

Our Path

Let
The awakened
Inner spirit set
The stage

To the clarity
Of all prevailing
Confusions and
Doubts

That is in
Nutshell is the
Challenge before

Let's roll up
The sleeves and
Go after
Freedom from
The stubborn
Ignorance

Otherwise,
We shall rot with
Its falsity,
Deception and
Greed only...

Challenge

Are we
Being trapped
Into this Nothing
Called,
"Universal Fat-egos"
Where hedonism is
The social norm
Or what

Is this the
Way mighty
Imposing their
Wills on poor and
Weak or not

Oh the
False reality of
The time where
The pseudo tribal
Claims begun
Calling the shots

In such a
Insane state,
How should we
Dare think, "Who
We're and what
We ought to be!"

Our
Truth

Essential
Humanity is a
Collective wisdom
That be ready to
Stand tall in
The turbulences
Of our time

It is our
Unity, dignity and to
Enjoy peace and hope
For children as well

Let the
Essential humanity
Be our truth and
Let it be the glow
In the dark

Let it
Inspire young
While we're
Fighting through
This one-time,
"Trial by existence..."

Let's
Begin

Clarity
Only window to
The beauty of the
Silent world

Once all
Illusions are
Emptied,
We're on the
Way to know,

"Who we're
And where's
The right path
To roll"

A path
Where
Awakening
Shall free us
From a long
Slumber

In the end
Its clarity
That shall
Open window
To our truth...

Be
Inspired

An illumined
Mind is the
Directedness to
Our big dream

Doesn't matter
How short or how
Long the trail,
Only finite life is
Biggest challenge
In-between

Let's
Move the needle
Forward to the
Infinite possibilities,

Let's
Battle out
The impossible task
And let "Goodness"
Be the directedness
To turn the dream
Into reality what we
Always want to be...

Lost

Of course,
Humans the
Link between
Known and the
Unknown

Yet
Miserably
Fails to grasp the
Significance of the
Noble Self in the
Turbulences of
Every age

For a long
He's been victim;
Bobbing into the
Stormy sea of anxiety
And fear and still not
Realizing his mighty
Inner strength...

Light & Shadow

Religion,
A remarkable
Preaching machine,
But lately losing
Grip over young
Of today

Rituals,
Prayers and
Worships don't
Mean much, if
Failed to change
The evil nature of
The believers

Look around
And witness why
For a long,
The world's been
Hand-cuffed in
Hatred, violence and
Million deaths and the
Beat goes on...

An
Appeal

Oh how I
Loved you
From the depths
Of my
Waited heart

I say,
Don't dismiss
My appeal
To be together
Once again

Come back
And know our
Loves still a
Burning candle
In the dark

Yes,
Come back and
Be the happy
We're once

Love, don't
Run away from
Your man... I am
The waiting dream
Of your life and laughs...

On
The Roll

Are we
Simply the
Dramatization of
Constant struggles
On the roll and
Nothing more than
That or what

Are we
Still in the
Search of
Freedom to point
Upward or we're
Rolling in the wrong
Direction or what

And
To that reality
Driven by the
Empirical thoughts
Is it an
Ephemeral memory
Or something else or
What!

Gift

What if
The world is but
A total abstraction
And that's where
We may know the
Truth

Indeed where
We can't elaborate
The issue in its full
Descriptive context
But a thriftiness of
Mathematical
Formulae

Abstractive
Capacity is a
Pure necessity,
Albeit a gift to be an
Enlightened being

Let's not
Run away from
Abstractions of God,
Being, life, truth and
Many mores to awaken
The spiritual soul of
The humanity itself...

Unfolding

Being
Caught
By the constant
Urge to know the
Self and the
World around,
So well

Perhaps
That is where
Much of his
Contemplative
Time is expended

Instead,
Human endeavor
With right
Purpose be the top
Priority

Yes,
To move the
Needle toward the
World we all wish
To live in...

Let's Welcome

Human
At time,
Feels being
Abandoned and
Loses self on the
Way, "What he
Ought to be"

Perhaps
He's distancing
From the very
Essence,
"Who he is"
May be unable to
Relate to the state
Of mind he's in

May be
He's silently
Asking to know his
Plight with reason
But not with
Pity at all

Let us
Honor his dignity
Let us cheer him with
Good understanding...

The Big Glow

As we keep
Walking
Along the
Rough terrain

We
Bring forth
Ideas and point of
Views; enriching
The world of
Meaning each time

It's the
World driven
By cognitive, emotive
And physical vibes taking
One step closer to the
Collective truth

Yes,
It's all about
Connectivity with
Others and to know
The totality of
What it is...

Judgment

Value
Judgment,
What a
Creative invention
Of the mind

Through
Time, it's been a
Measure of human
Conduct all right

Then there is
The issue of
Subjectivity adding
To the complexity
Already is there

Value
Judgment always
A challenge when torn
Between subjective and
Objective game of the
Trial by existence...

Reflections

We're
The wonderful
Spirits and we
Grow and change
While pursuing
Our collective truth

At times,
We're walking along
A right track and often
The dark for a long

Come,
Let's evolve from
Confined perceptions
To innovate the
Unbridle consciousness

Let's dare to
Go from the known to
The Unknown while
We've this one chance...

Either It Is,
Or It Is Not

I am
The holographic
Projection who
Is nothing but discreet
Thoughts flickering
For a brief

I am
The soul albeit
My will guiding I
To the total reality,
"What is?"

I alone is
The constant
In this holistic
Memories, births and
Rebirths and

Of course,
I got to be a moral
Necessity to be free
From the make-belief,
"Conceptuality of
All that is..."

Blueprint

What is an
Enlightened
Mind be
Understood first
Before probing
The Self and
The world

Yes, to be
A new reality
Where
The inner being
Emanates moral
Drive and rational
Insight

And at that
Turning point,
Let the being
Explore and
Actualized

The
Anticipated
Noble mission that
Has been already
Defined way before...

Gist

Reality
What we know
Is subjective
Thoughts, words
And deeds brewing
Into the
Rational matrix,
I suppose!

Lack of
Understanding
Means
Many unknown
Consequences
To face thereof

If existence
Is purely contextual
Why do we think,
"We've freedom?"

Perhaps
Life just
An image into the
Mirror of million
Unknowns where
The endless cycle of
Births and deaths rule
The connected beings...

Tears & Blunders

The issue before
Our thick heads is,
"How do we regain
Sincerity of purpose
To reach the final goal
Before it's too late"

How do we
Convince billion others,
"We're born with a
Meaning in this world"

Here we're
Pushing forward through
The twenty-one and not yet
Well evolved to measure-up
To our collective worth

Whence
All struggles, violence's
Deaths and destructions
Keep chipping off our
Genuine humanity
Each time...

Creative
Will

Go where
No other has
Thought to be

Go where
No starlight has
Reached us today

Let it
Be the
Daring creative
Imagination to
Explore the world
Beyond

Let it
Be the
Glowing spirit
In you to know,
The power within

Be bold to
Believe in your
Determined will,
"How to fly off
Anywhere you
Wish to be... "

Missing!

Thought,
I'll never arrive
At the
Point of knowing,
"Who am I?"

Is that
I've accidently
Landed into this
Uncertainty or what!

In such a
Chaotic milieu, I've
Become my lingering
Past and the present
Where I hold fading
Memories as well

No idea,
Where future shall
Direct my meaning
But the journey
Rolls on toward the
Unity only...

Be
Free

What is the
Rationale to be
Human
If he fails to
Know his blatant
Truth

Where's
The intelligent
Human who dares
To question
Falsity of his belief
That fails to correct
The myopic claims

What's the
Point in holding
Something
That lacks
Moral dignity of
Humans and fails to
Preach Goodness
To entire whole...

Amnesia

We're
The point of
Relationship with
All others

We're the
Potential truth
Always and

Still we're
Unable to
Reform the weak
Societal issues of
Our time

What a
Paradox, while
We live in the age of
Information and still
We're ignorant

We know
Certain aspect of
Our beliefs may not be
Rational, but we simply
Go on with 'em
So sheepishly...

Res-
Possibility

If this is
Essential
Humanity,
In that case,
It is not
Perfect yet

For one
Thing, there is
A need of clarity,
If the
Set goal to be
Understood well

There is
Also a need to
Clean-up the
Thick layers of
Greed and

Of course,
War mongering
Old habits of us,
Who are the real
Culprits indeed...

The Crux

Love,
What an eternal
Gift
That brings
Happiness and
Struggles
At the same time

Life
What a magic
Joining every born
With death in time

Quest,
Too what an opp
To make it through
With a meaning
Or two

Time,
What a
Sneaky flow
From known
To the unknown,
Always...

First
Principle

**Let
Human Essence
Be the first principle
To tackle all the
Teasing unknowns
Of the time ever**

**Let
Awareness
Sustain the power
Of mysticism
Forever**

**Time to
Get smart and
Know, "Where is
The right path
To roll from this
Point on?"**

**Though,
We exists in a
Conceptual
Contradiction;
Keep on exploring
Even Mr. Death
Says, "Hello!"**

Apodictic

Oh the
Cognitive
Perplexity
What a magic
Taking "I" from
Her to beyond

It got to be
That drive called,
"I" taking to the
World where
'Am drawn

It's the
Curiosity and
Determined will
Pressing "I"

To fly
Off the edge and
Be the unity from
Beginning to
Beginning...

Starlight's

Wherever
Intelligent beings
Inhabit the Universe

There got to be
Noble souls holding
Their
Rational direction

Let them
Hold their inner
Strength to explore,
To know and to
Understand their
Meaning

Let
The starlight's
Guide us earthly
Beings our defined
Destiny
Before reality
Disappears from
Our moral
Sparkling thoughts...

I, Roll

Things
That I don't see
And, the thoughts
That hasn't emerged,
On the scene yet

Leads I to
Affirm there is another
Meaning beyond

Dreams
May not be the reality
Yet they're inspirations
To our existence

Life,
Not so perfect still
The base from where
I catapulted to the unknown
With power of my will

Time,
Ain't real, but I
Roll along with it
From the past into
Present and do
Begin to rethink of
My waiting future 'cause
All possibilities is "I am"

Theme

When lyrics
Fits the sound,
The consequential
Listener got to be
So happy every time

What if,
The singer fails to
Justify its meaning
Do listeners throw away
The creation or what!

What if
Essential humanity
Is so enlightening
At the core and
Still, fails to convince
The whole, I mean how
Do we clear the deck?

The
Way

Self-sufficient
Examination may
Open-up the window
To an experience
Called,
"Ideal Life"
In an instant

Otherwise,
Being caught
In the empirical
Existence shall be
Struggling forever

I mean.
In the latter case,
There is a
Nagging subjectivity,
Chaos and unfulfilled
Expectations to face
Between birth and
Death simply

Let us learn,
"How to grasp the
Genuine reality where
Love, friendship and
Truth is waiting to
Welcomes all...

Art,
Forever

Oh the magic
Of art what a
Dancing aphrodisiac
Albeit a restless state of
The creative mind

Always taking us
To the realm of
Beauty and ugly
Places at the same
Time

Art is a wonderful
Aesthetic experience
It's an abstractive
Adventure and it even
Drops us into the world
Of hardships and tears
As well

Oh the magic of
Creative art such an
Immortal blueprint;
Expressing music,
Paintings, poetica and the
Scientific thoughts on an
Equal footings......

Be
Real

Why do we
Need identity,
I mean in the
Metaphysical sense!

Any ways,
Why care to be
An authentic being
In the
World of disorder

Again,
Whats
The worth of
This individual
Freedom

I mean,
How does
It fit into
This contextual
Existence where
We've been nothing,
But mere
Approximations!

Oscillations

Oh the
Ambiguities
Swinging the
Restless mind
From one end
To another while
Questioning
Reality itself

In such a
Constant state of
Debates, doubts and
Failed direction
How can he escape
From any change and
Chaos of his time?

Yes, from the
Realm of his
Contradictions,
Confusions and
Assumptions
To know his long
Awaited truth!

Identity

If being is
The subjective
Consciousness
Should that mean
He's in the world
Of inferences only

What if
His presence is a
Moral drive; governing
The ultimate simply

On glimpsing
Into the mirror
Of life and time,
Is he not the
One, who thinks,
"Being always,
Thought to be"

Human,
What an inseparable
Conceptual belief and
Mystical abstraction,
Substratum...

Magic Window

Look at the
Brand new us
Every day and
Every
Whichever way

In such a
Inspiring state
There is
Neither birth nor
Death, but the
Irresistible force
To roll forward

It may well be
Absurd to think of
Infinity from a finite
Three-pound organic
Machine

But that's the
Only window letting
To fulfill curiosities,
Imaginations and be
Worthy, "Who we're..."

Unio Mystico

And there is
Possibility within
The thinking
Being

It's
Far and beyond
Human imaginations
And yet paradoxically
Nearest to the core

Indeed,
It's the very real
Inner being whose
An evolving infinity
Yet to be understood
So-well...

Open
Journey

Don't wait
'Till it's too late
To say,
"Gee I missed
My train today"

Let
Self-realization
Leads to the place
Where you never
Have to say, "Sorry"

Let it be
The new journey
To be the power
Within to make it
Through the
Complex reality
As is

Let you
Enter the world
Where Perceptuality
Is the abstraction of
The silent soul indeed...

Let's
Dance

Let's
Tango to the
Music called,
"Best lovers in the
World"

Let's
Dance
Cheek-to-cheek
To be never
Separated ever
Again

Yes, darling,
Let's
Keep dancing
To be meaningful
Two souls;
Bonded as one

Let's
Dance to the
Music of joy and
Be the best lovers in
The world...

Big Cage

In
The deep
Structured reality
There is nothing,
But ephemeral
Experiences only

In such a
Grand scene;
Human is a
Spider trapped into
An ever chaotic web

Nothing,
But confinement;
Stifling his
Adventures and

There is
Urgency
To escape from
The cage at once...

Synergy

Humanity
What a glowing
Synergy driven by the
Past, present and the
Future to be

Humanity
What a flow of
Thoughts and actions
Through challenges
Time after time

Humanity,
What a constant
Grief and joy
Humanity,
What a struggle
To stay alive

Humanity
What a
Necessity torn
Between
Life and death

Humanity,
What an abstruse
Concept, it is...

Self-Thought

Given
Complexity of
All that is
Why does he
Demand,

A priori
Categories,
To clarify the
Fuzzy vision
He holds

Is it from
Such a premise,
He can grasp,
"How far he is from
The base reference
Of his truth"

Is that
The way,
Is he free and
Ready to take
The moral action as
His first call or what!

Half-n-Half

Funny
It is
Human nature
That shuttlecocks
Between right and
Wrong, between
Good and evil
And between
Love and hate

Well,
There emerges
The issue of the
Subjective judgment,
"How to justify the
Objective outcome"

Perhaps
That's why the
Journey of the spirit
Remains,
"Half-and-half" and
Surprisingly no
Regret, yet to report..."

Power
Within

**Morality
Not an
Utopian thought,
Not to be
Read in books**

**Morality
Not an exclusive
Claim
Of any other**

**Albeit
Morality
What a positive
Force of
Stability and
Harmony of
The whole**

**Morality
Always a healer
Of the insane
Human mind
For sure...**

Reality

Never forget,
"We're
Mere possibilities
Who've arrived for
A brief

In that case,
It's worth noting,
There's no lasting
Freedom, Divine or
Whatever, but in
The conceptual mind

Oddly in such
A scenario, we're
Nameless, deathless
And no conscious
Judgment to be
Previleged and

The eternal
Cycle of
Birth and rebirth
Keeps spinning, yet
Remains constant

I mean,
Once our
Thoughts leaves
There is only
Nothingness: as was,
As is and shall be..

The Passage

Each to play
His/her part to
Build a reality out
Of the lofty dreams

Each got to
Be good not
Today, but for the
Very necessity of
Tomorrow too

We're
Running out of
Time for the entropy
Is rapidly on the rise
And the noble goal
Seems far everyday

We're
Here to build a
World of meaning,
Harmony and hope

Yes,
To bring forth our
Beauty and truth,
"Who we're and
What we ought to be..."

The
Essence

What "I" is
Just the reality of
My essence

Indeed,
A being whose
Emanating thoughts,
And indefatigable will to
Make some difference
Before the times up

Of course,
What "I" just is
A mere spark into the
Totality of all that I try
To decipher in my time

Given all the
Facts of my identity,
Must I lower
Neither dignity nor
Must I seek pity?

"I "exist to
Set the mission
Though a brief
Moment to shine...

Sacred
Vows

We've been
Dancing in the
Dream for a long

Now, darling
It's time to face
The real issues of
Our friendship

We've been
Teasing each for
A while, but darling
It's the time to
Face the ultimate
Truth now

Come,
Let's be true and
Roll the wheels of
Love all the way to
The realm, where we
Shall never be apart

I say,
"Darling be bold
And be honest and take
The eternal vows to be
A renewed experience:
Love forever, forever...
Forever at last..."

Self-Cause

What
Drives us to
Be the best and
Still dare
Hold-on to our
Destiny is that

Life itself is
The one chance
To make it through
With an awakened
Soul, simply

What
An inspiring
Experience
When we're
Not afraid and

We keep the
Journey rolling
Even when the
Odds are many...

The Core

On entering
The challenging
Domain of the
Ethical ideal

We soar
To the Highest
Reaches of our
Noble virtues

We're
Reborn with
Moral insight and
Rational grasp,
"What we ought
To be"

Only when
We dare reach
To the noble inner
Being at the core

That is
When we're
The Truth,
Possibility and
Freedom albeit

We're
The overture:
Immortal Essence
And no question raised...

Inner Call

Folks kept
Dancing whole night
To salute the new
Spirit of kindness

Folks kept
Singing with one
Voice though they
Spoke different lings

Folks
Agreeing, "It's time
To come together and
Rid off the war-mongers
From the scene"

They even
Agreed to save the
Future of their kids
As one global family,
Indeed

Folks kept
Reverberating
The blue skies,
"Let Peace, Harmony
And Hope rule the
Whacky world..."

Believe

In the midst
Of a stygian night
Where nothing but
The silence governs
The experience

In such a
Solemn milieu,
I dare stand with
A stare toward
The glorious
Skies

Where
Infinite stars
Keep firing-up
My determination
Letting I to walk
Through the dark

That is
An inspiration
To my freewill;
Allowing I
To keep rolling
Along the trail
Where I wish to be...

Endless Trail

We've
Won the battle,
Didn't we?

We've
Done impossible
Possible
Haven't we?

We've
Arrived at the gate
Of our big dream,
Didn't we?

So many
Inconclusive cross
Roads to pass from
One generation to
Another and

The journey
Seems bunch of
Brief victories now
And then and
The trail never ends...

Gauntlet

What if
Truth is an
Inner projection
Of the intelligent
Mind forever

And what if
It's an ever
In conclusion
Between,
"What is and
What is not?"

And
This logic, this
Individuation,
This broad vision
And hunger for
Freedom,
"What
Is it all for! "

That is the
Gauntlet thrown at
Subjective state of
The human mind and
The struggle still
Remains...

Time
To Roll

Why keep
Walking through a
Winding trail and
Not knowing where
Will it end?

Why be
Caught into a
Situation where real
Meaning is missing
From the equation

Why be
Lost into the dark
When billion stars are
Ready to guide

Human,
The innovative, the
Creative and the very
Rational to be

Why
He still keeps
Walking through
The dark...

My
Point

"I" is the
Journey leading
To the realm of
My waiting goal

Yes as
I am, the
Well determined
Will to explore the
Self and the world,
In toto

After all,
"What else
May be the point
Being born in
Human form"

I probe
The riddles of
All That Is
Through lyrics to
Know my meaning

Who cares?
Either 'am right or
Wrong...so long I am
Sincere with my
Trial by Existence...

Being
As Is

While
Measuring your
Worth be sure to
Know, "You
Alone can inspire
Million others
In return"

Indeed,
Your moral being
Can only bring
Tolerance, love and
Hope whence a
Greater cohesion
To the whole

That is
The essence of
Unity, liberty and
Humanity of your
Noble Soul...

Global
Force

As challenges
Of our time keeps
Piling-up by the
Minutes

Why don't
We take a bold
Stand to resolve
"Em head-on

Enough
Thinking, planning
And debating for a
Long

Let each
Take the micro-
Responsibility and
Do the job on a
Consistent basis

Only
Individual global
Citizen is the
Answer and let
Divine be left alone in
His celestial splendors...

In Love

Love
What a dice
Thrown into the
Throbbing two hearts
Of uncertainty

If it
Hits the reality
In their favor
They won the game,
In an instant

If not,
Tears and deep
Wounds shall endure
For some time

That's the
Consequence of
Their joint destiny
Called, "Love"

Oh that a
Magic to bear
Called, "Love"
And what a risk
They can't avoid,
But to fall in love
Time and time again...

Trans-
Formation

Let's draw
Order of truth to
Touch the genuine
Humanity within

Let
All irrational
Beliefs and their
False narratives
Be dismissed,
At once

In the
Same vein,
Let's learn,
"How to transform
From stubborn
Separateness to the
Metaphysical unity
As the first step..."

Great Pursuit

"We're
The sum
Total of reality"
Let it be the
Premise

We
Can query
Million riddles;
Orbiting our
Restless minds, but
Then we may be
Kidding ourselves

We think
We're the
Ideal- world of
Being ever good,
But we're not yet,
"The Perfect Being..."

Ethics

Is it not time
Each is obliged
To be mindful of
His/her conduct

Is it not time
Each to take
Responsibility and
Begin the mission

Is it not time
Each to prevent
Bigotry, violence,
Asinne bloodsheds,
At least

Is it not time
To think of the
Future of our kids

Is it not time
To relearn, "How
Should I be a friend
Rather than being
A foe!"

The Process

Almost daily,
We witness
Never-ending drama
Where relational dialogues
Keep jostling for a dominant
Position in the instability
Of human reality we're in

In such a
Societal gymnastics,
Good folks
Either absorbs such
Silent tough-of-wars
Between fat-egos
Or they do rebel and
Set the fire on

From such
Turmoil's, sometime
Good triumphant
And the world moves
Ahead

We call it,
"Historic Process"
And such adventures
Facilitate in advancing
Along a right track!

Missing
Variables

If life is
So sweet why
Young are dying
In the shadows of
Fear and anxiety

If love is
So sweet, why
There're million
Tragic tales

If human is
So smart, why is
He is so insecured
Of the future today

If
Techno-nonbeing
Is evolving so fast,
Why the natural
Human is not

If religion was
So sacred, why
There is no lasting
Peace in the world!

We're

Being though a
Rational instinct
And moral will,
Why he's in ever
Suspension and not
Willing to change

If he's a
Transformational
Agent; evolving from
Sense-perception to
The "Silence in deep"
Why is he not sure
Of the journey
To the end

Being
What... all the
Possibilities, curiosities
And ability to ask
Million questions
And still
Be unaware of
His metaphysical
Fingerprints ...

A Survey

Reality
May be an
Interplay of
Consciousness with
Object and change

It's the
Change against
The unchanged where
Paradoxes, riddles and
Chaos keep dancing
On the scene

In-between
There swirls myth,
Superstation and divinely
Notion; failing to
Fulfill the expectation

And the
Consequence:
Intelligent being
Keeps dancing
Between, "What is
And what is not?"

The
Mode

There is a
Steady search,
"How to be
A Perfect Being
In the world" and

There is a
Struggle to grasps,
"Conceptual truth
With inclusion of
Metaphysical
Necessity" as well

So long,
These are not
Reconciled,
"Perfection"
Remains on hold

Time to
Wake-up from the
Slumber soon

Time to be the
Determined will
To meet the elusive
Truth...

A
Necessity

What
Human subject
Need is the sense of
Responsible conduct

Only then
He emerges
As his own strength

In that case,
Morality awakes
In him and the
Real journey is on

Let him
Be aware of his
Personhood and
Be the wave-maker
In the world...

Great
Leap

Is it
Not time,
We refine
The old habits;
Paving the path
To be good again

If
Human is
Good at the core,
Why ignore the
Positive from within

Let us
Come together
And begin a
New dialogue
And act to be one
Meaningful voice
For a change

Let the
Solemn conscience
Free us from the
Inglorious seven-sin...

Blurred
Vision

There is
Infinite
Wisdom build
Over time

Of course,
In the name of
Fair justice,
Peace and security
To name a few

In spite,
Our kind keeps
Spinning-up
Myriad whims in
Every direction, but
Staying the course

No wonder, we've
Not seen through
The foggy vision, the
Clarity of reality yet...

The Force

Unity, validity
And identity
Be at the top
While chugging
Along this track
Called,
"Life and time"

Common-sense
And reason should
Guide, but them
Demand willingness
To act every time

Let the
Infinite vigor and
Endless imaginations
Open the way

Let there
Emerge a
Success story and
Let humanity
Continue the journey
Toward enlightenment...

Headwinds

Ethics be
The overture:
Either
Right or wrong
Or what

Against
Such a backdrop,
Why keep judging
Between austerity
And hedonism when
We don't have the
Right mindset

Wonder,
What if we lost
Something precious
While walking
Through the dark
For a long!

A
Perspective

What if
We're the last
Link left in the
Mighty Universe
Who can think:
Love, life, time, truth
And even the divine
Or whatever else

What if
We're
The final bead
Into the cosmic chain
Where we're,
"Being Becoming"

What if
We're the last
Intelligent entity
Soon to be vanished into
"Nothingness," I mean
From our conceptual
Meaning of all that
We care to know so well...

Think
Right

All beliefs
Be resolved soon
For only one
Moral principle
To be welcomed

That be the
Basis upon which
To build a better
Humanity of trust,
Dignity and grace

Or else,
The world would
Remain divided and
Rot into a
Constant conflict
To the ugly end

All differences
Be resolved and let's
Begin a nova attitude
To be in harmony, peace
And the inclusion ...

Miracle

The Self
Alone is the
"Universal
Consciousness"

For it
Opens the
Sealed door to the
World of myriad
Unknowns yet to be
Understood

Let Self
Emerge as the
Positive force
To keep steady on
The road

The Self,
What a creative
Communicator for
Its own good

And verily,
The Self what
An eternal power
To know,
"All that is..."

Equation, Incomplete

Ethics
And the Self,
Sometimes they
Coincide and
Sometimes they
Don't

That is the
Hidden struggle
Beneath every
Planned quest

While
Half way
Through the
Pursuit
Being is also
Troubled by the
Separateness:

Between
Conceptual
Reality and
Metaphysical
Necessity and

There
Oscillates the
Meaning without
A definite intention!

Meditation

How do
We justify our
World view
When things are
Not in control

That's been
The spinning
Concern for
Sometimes

Wonder,
"What is the
Ultimate aim
We've
Been seeking
To comprehend!

Is it either
To know it while
In life or to be
Grasped beyond!

Recollection

Once
We're all
Five fingers so
Tightly held together
By love, ambition and
Constant struggles

In time,
Each left the nest
And landed
In an alien culture,
Then

And of course,
New experiences and
Hard work paid off
Each to meet the
Career goals in time

Meanwhile
Loving mom and
Pop left the world
And soon after all
My caring siblings

Well, here
I am today
Mulling over,
"Either was it worth
It all or having lost
All the pure loved ones..."

Creative
Being

Being
Cause of
Thoughts that
Evolves ion
Myriad perspectives
To gauge the world
While he's in the
Game

Being
Defining his
Personhood
With some wisdom
And self-confidence
Keeps rolling
Forward through
Life and time

That be
His objectified
Essence and that be
His existence...what is
The First Principle,
"He ought to be..."

The
Way

To these
Discreet tiny
Bubbles called,
"Stream of human
Consciousness;"
Revealing the
World of unknown

They are
Verily expressions
Of the cosmic reality
That we've been riding
Them for a while

Time
To know the
Depth of our inner
Being and

Let's
Begin changing
From the state of
Quasi-animal to the
Enlightened Truth...

Big Image

Humanity,
What a giant
Organic bubble
Always an
Unstable whole

Humanity
Driven by
Time, belief, values,
Relations and so on
What a big dance
Full of uncertainty
In action

Humanity,
What a mixed bag
Where either
Understanding or
Misunderstanding
Defining judgment,
Freedom and change

Humanity,
What an
Ever exploding
Synergy spinning with
Million
Unanswered dreams...

Last
Chance

Is it true?
Each born human
Is an interpretational
Dimension of the
Life experience or
What!

What if,
Each born being
"Societal Inspiration"
To lift the young to
The greater heights

Well,
The issue is,
"Do each human
Born knows the
Significance of
His/her moral call
Or not..."

Road
To Sanity

Without
Reason and moral
Goodness, we can't
Claim we've arrived
At the gate

Time
To refine the
Religion itself where
Harmony with others
Is emphasized over
Myopia and phobia

Time
To clear the passage
Toward enlightenment
With a new
Understanding,

"There be one
Nameless religion;
Inspiring to live in
Peace with compassion
And not be hung-up with
The brand names..."

Core
Principles

Let's grasp
The core conception,
"Who we're and what
We ought to be"

Let it be the
Primary principle
To take the first step
To be strong with
The creative vibes:

Cognitive,
Emotive and
Physical to interact
With others for good

Let it be
The Equal principle,
"How to build a world
Of right vision,
Harmony, dreams and
Of course with the
Moral confidence..."

Love,
Eternal

Our
Scripts been
Written
In the name
Of eternity and
We can't escape
The set destiny

Darling, it's a
Tall order to
Fulfill but that's
The only way to be
In love forever

I mean darling,
This is our moment
To seize, "Who we're
And how deep is
Our trust!"

Yes,
Darling that's
La amore eterna
That's our truth and
That we must believe
It forever while in
Love...

"I"

"I"
Excels in the very
Continuity of my
Spiritual
Consciousness

Where "I"
Just a projection
"Either here
Or over there"

My presence
Here is empirical
But the thoughts keep
"I" in the realm beyond

Whatever
The case may be,
Let "I" be
The real humanity
While am here
For a brief

Let
"I" be the
Embodiment of
Simplicity and goodwill
While transiting from
Here to eternity...

Glow
In Dark

In human,
Purity of
Holistic experience
Must be at the core

If at all, he
Can live in the
Mystical state where
No distinction between
Subject-object relation
Exists

That is
Where his truth
Waits and that is
Where he shall be
The total bliss

Let
His "Moral Self"
Be the glow while
Passing through the
Dark...

Quest

Why
Be alive
Upon the notion,
"Nothingness"

Well,
What does it
Mean in the world
Still in turmoil

Is it
Being trapped
Into the world of
Boredom or no
Imagination at all

"Nothingness"
Either a unique
"Self-Thought "or
Just an intellectual
Escapism from it all!

Nemesis

When
Believers close
Their minds and stay
Silent from critically
Looking at the belief
That has betrayed 'em
For a very long; it is
A sad story to tell
The world so openly

How should
They address the
Wrong doings and
Wake-up to the
Modern reality and be
The enlightened beings

What if
Divinely truth is
Accepted without
A rational grasp,

How long the
State of ignorance
Should go on?
How long
They be silent when
Million children
Seems caught into the
Flames: hatred, revenge
And senseless killings...

Doppelganger

Being
Caught between
Opinion and
Truth

Former
Everybody's
Owners , but the
Latter,
Got no individual
Possessor yet

Opinions
Are ephemeral,
But the truth is an
Everlasting teaser

Surprisingly,
Human
Is the blend
Of opinion and
Truth and

Let the passion
Of his soul dictate
The bold journey
Toward the camp
Called, "Truth."

Conceptual
Clarity

Human
Who is the very
Essence,
"What he thinks. What
He believes and what
Conclusions he derives...."

He's the
Continuum change;
Rejuvenating
Every now and then
And not even
Budging to win
The game

That is the
Journey of a brave
Spirit who's heading
Toward Uncertainty,
But driven by the
Certainty of his own
Determined will...

Flashes

What's
This reality that
We seek to know
With immense
Curiosity

Are we the
Lone being in
The universe,
Standing upon
Sense perception and
Introspection or what!

What is the
Meaning of existence,
If we're not the
Masters of the plan

How do we
Know complexity
Of reality with
Reason and a
Moral vision and
Go in action,
"How we ought to be."

Silent
Stream

Oh the
Silent stream
Meandering
Through soft
And rough terrain
While on the way
To the mighty blue Sea

How
She encounters
Million obstacles,
Deadly storms and
Endless human abuses
But her journey rolls
Toward the blue Sea

That is the
Power of the silent
Stream so inspiring
To our world

That is the
Magic of the
Silent stream
Keeping life alive
And well while on her
Way to the blue Sea...

Journey,
Cut Short

Human
At times,
Obsessed by the
Fever of ego,
Wealth and fame

Along the
Way,
Transforming
Himself from
Being real to be
The fake smile only

The world
Adores him for
Money and bows
Down to his prestige

In the end,
Where there
Is no integrity,
The game lasts for
A limited time only....

Rejuvenation

When
Misjudgment,
Distorts the
Meaning of
Human freedom

There
Inevitably
Emerges
Protests, riots
Bloodsheds and
Even deaths on
The scene

Such is the
Consequential
State of many
Societal issues
Of our time

Such is the
Process of fine
Tuning the wrongs

And such is the
Courage of people
Willing to die in the
Name of their freedom...

Unity

Either real or
Imaginary shall be
Reduced to nothingness
Through the impersonal
Time that we know
So well

All humanity
Too shall be reduced
To the ultimate will;
Nothing to seek but
Harmony and Peace
Only in return

All that dust
Spinning in the
Human mind shall
Also end when humans
Are in the zone named,
"Global Unity"

Before
Leaving
Individual urn
Behind

Let us
For a big
Change, change
Our human nature
And gift the world of
Meaning, hope and
Truth to the kids...

Walk

Let
Conscience keep
Demanding an
Intuitive will to act in
The name of good always

From
Such a fountain of
Inner strength,
Let being arise with a
Moral courage and
Takes the first step

A step to
Absorb the complexities
Of all there is with the
Mighty rational insight

And remember,
Only few have broken
The glass ceilings and
Billions still struggling
Against their head-winds...

Being &
Essence

Human
Making of choices
Define the very act
Of his freedom

Only
In such a mode of
Reality, human has a
Meaning to be
Only
In such a set-up,
Human is his moral
Existence simply

Only
In such a frame of
Reference, human
Is the hero and

Keeps rolling
All the way to the
Glorious trail that
Never ends....

Beauty & Truth

Beauty and
Truth always
Best inspirations
To live a worthy
Life

Beauty and
Truth what a real
Manifest freewill
Even while
Walking through
The dark tunnel

Be the spirit
With courage
And keep walking
As if you're the
Brilliant light only

Let all
Trivialities reduce
To nothing and let you
Be the
"Beauty and Truth
While walking toward
Your eternity...

Inner Being

Don't
Dismiss human
Being merely a
Flesh and blood

For he's
Never a docile
Spirit floating
Between
Birth and death

In fact,
He's the creative
Unity within the
Complexity of all
That is

He's
An awakened
Being dancing with
The issues of
His time

Human
Who's the
Architect of his
Conceptual reality
Still suspended into the
State of uncertainty...

Reflective

Salute to
The reflective art
Albeit, what is the
Very gift of every
Human being
Born

If it's
Sustained over
A long time,
Well he has earned
His license to explore
From the self to the
Totality-of-human-
Experience here
And beyond

That is
Where he's supreme
That is when he knows,
"He's conquered the
Mind"

I mean, that is
How he becomes
Larger than life for
Knowing, "He's the gift
Of the reflective art
Himself for sure..."

Be Smart

Rage and
Anxiety bubbling
Up now and then
Not knowing the
Cause sometimes

If the
Milieu keeps
Feeding fear out
Of ignorance

In that case
The source be
Tackled
Accordingly,
Of course

Existence
Is not a free
Experience and
Never a fair game

Strengthening
Inner being is the only
Way to make it through
The recurring storms...

Scope &
Hope

Everyone
Is a potential
Energy after all

But, in life
Must learn how
To unleash it to
Set the noble goals

Be sure
Never to budge
From the moral
Stand on facing any
Challenge on-hand

Let
Each being
Be the hero for
Preserving his truth
Yes, while
Walking along
The highway of million
Possibilities as well...

Glow & Flares

An inevitable
Force of human
Is to abstract
Essence from the
Complex reality,
Always

And, to that
Bold adventure, we
Call, "The Quest
Toward the logical
Mind"

A quest
That is an open
Ended where
Million opinions
Either scientific or
Mystics collide to
Make some sense

And that's how
The cycle of knowing
Continues sometimes
Quite brilliantly and
Sometimes quite aimless...

The
Mirror

Intelligent being
Who's the owner of
His thoughts thus
Can move the mighty
Mountains may not be
Good enough

If he lacks
The moral will and a
Rational insight when
The real challenge is on

That is the
Dilemma
Of the modern
Human and that
Is the issue facing
Him every day today

Intelligent being
Who is the live image
into the mirror of
Reality; fails to identity
Himself and the time
Mercurially rolls on...

"I"
Exist

"I" means,
I exist to know
The moral Self
That I am

If not
Today but before
Saying, 'Avoir"
To the world

That is
My hope and
That is
My endeavor
To the end

"I " means
I exist to take
A leap forward
To justify,

"What is the
Meaning having
Born human?"

Our
Call

Why do we
Forget, "We're the
Moral possibility and
Rational judgment"

I mean,
"Why not begin to
Rethink of a new future
Where we can achieve
Our ultimate being
Without facing any
Pseudo assumption"

Let's not
Forget, "We're the
Descendants of goodwill
And courage to shape
An awakened destiny than
We've ever imagined..."

Magic
Wand

Depiction
Of what is and what
Is not is the magic of
The innovative art

It may be
Either "Verbal or
Abstractive "but doesn't
Matter for it demands
Reinterpretation
Every time

Oh yes
These creative arts:
Music, painting or a
Poetica always teasing
The world of thoughts

Of course,
It is a great escape
From the rigidity and
The false narratives
We hear every day

Art, what a
Wonderful gift of
To touch the shores of
The world beyond...

Gateway

At the Creative
Gate way where
New imaginations,
New Possibilities and
The fired-up spirits
Collide always

Let 'em lifts
Humanity to the
Universal
Understanding,
Tolerance and dignity
Of the whole

Let 'em
Be the
Rhythm, melody
And meaning and

Let 'em keeps
Knocking the
Creative Gateway
As a necessity;
Explore ring their
Wonderful minds...

Prime
Keys

Amid these
Irregularity of
Quotidian chores

Why don't
We drop
Trivialities and
Get away
From the dark

Instead,
Why not be the
Single Super Glow
Called, "Good"

Why not
Redefine our
Common destiny

What is the
Enduring peace,
Harmony and genuine
Moral meaning...

Forever

Dear Heart,
We're dreamers
We're lovers and
Challenges are but
Petite steps to us

I say, let
The dream
Turns into reality
And let our story
Begins and evolves
Via ours to come

Dear Heart,
It was your
Sweet smile that
Kicked off the journey
We've been on

That is
The memory I hold
As a purity of my best
Human experience

And that is the way
We shall sail through
Eternity being one
Love forever...

Ephemeral

Mystic
And scientific
Conclusions keep
Arriving
On an equal level
All right

There is no
Certainty, but only
Probabilities and
Randomness to be
The fact of reality
Where we're in

All is nothing
But an ephemeral
Conceptuality
And the validity of
"Absolutism" faded
Sometime ago

It is
The core essence
Where creativity
Sparks and thought
Evolves, but the deep
Complexity remains...

Will to
Ascend

While
Slumbering
Through
Hedonistic habits
And caged by the
Techno-aphrodisiac

It appears,
Lately
We've forgotten
The very moral
Perspective; failing
To see the right
Direction

We're the
Embodiment
Of all possibilities
And, why are we
Lost while on our
Way to conquor
The mind!

But,
Why?

Knowing
All-That-Is to be
The abstract unity

Must be
Very epiphany
Albeit
An intuitive
Spontaneity

That be the
Right journey
Leading toward
Truth

Why then
In time, we've
Forgotten that very
Spark of awakening?

And why
We're failing
To pay attention
To the very missing
Equation...

The Big Grasp

God
Just another
Conceptual spark
That invokes nothing
But self-consciousness
In return

That is
In essence, when
Human and the
Divine becomes one
And there is no
Difference

That is
The state of an
Illumined mind who
Understands, "Who he is
And what he is for..."

That is
The fearless being
Who is aware,
"He is the participant
In the totality of all
There is" and therefore
He is truly a free spirit...

Validation

All flowing
Serenely
Through this
Magnifique
Beauty and truth

That is the
Solemn spirit of
Us
Please
Don't disturb
It's meditative
State

Don't let
The glorious
Bliss fades from
The experience

Let our
Gracious souls
Roll forward to
The meaning in
Time...

The
Walker

Only
Unity is to
Set a right story of
Every walker on
The scene

Who's
Seeking
His/her truth
To be understood
Before the times up

No point
In suffering from
Regret, remorse or
Guilt
Let only intention
Be to know, "How
To be a worthy being"

Storms,
Thunders and
Heavy pours shall
Come and go, but
Let him/her know,
"There is always a
Sunrise at the end."

Open
Book

Where
Intuition, reason
And vision coincides,
A deep insight is
A big reward

Let us
Open a book
Where-in all good
Thoughts are printed:

To move the
Mountains
Via our collective
Action

Let us
Emerge as the
Single juggernaut
Force of change and

Let it
Help in finishing the
Book with meaningful
Conclusions...

Silent
Steps

Being
Caught into
The complex
Matrix of
Perpetually
Contradicting
Reality

Seems,
We've been
Blinded by the
Glaring blunders;
Defacing the
"Self-Identity"

Well, I say
That is
The time to ascend
With a will to win

And that is
When we must
Keep walking
Through the thick
And thin...

Justification

It's
A posteriori
Necessity

Let human
Embattle the
Constant
Riddles, conflicts
And mysteries to
Justify his pursuits

No point
To be living into
The world of
No change, no new
Thought or listening
To the same old
Divisional rhetoric's

Instead let us
Look upward
Toward the infinite
Possibilities and

Let us
Be inspired by the
Great minds that 've
Shown the way many
Times before...

Happy Mother's Day

In her
Firmness there
Was deep
Sincerity and
The power of
Courage

In her
Thoughts
There was much
Willingness
To do good

Oh yes,
She was the lifter
Of the lost spirits
Who needed the most

She's a lady
Who sacrificed
Whatever she had
And that solemn soul,
Is my dear mother
Indeed forever...

Endless

And the
Time is here to
Know nothing is
Forever

No name,
No material gains
And no ambition
Can last ever

It's a
Reality of
Beginning and end,
Yet eternally keep
Returning

In such
A giant spinning
Wheel of
All we know

Human is
Born, living for
Brief and falls in the
Open arms of Death;
Reentering other
Universe time and
Time again...

Reflection

Don't know
"What is my
Existential Truth"

Instead, I am
Aware, "My inner
Being that must
Be a positive
Outcome of Good"

If the
Sum total of it
Manifests in all
Humans as one mighty
Force of moral
Willingness

Inevitably each
Soul shall evolve from
Imperfection to the
Perfection and

At that
Very instant,
"Humanity shall manifest
As its own Truth."

Self-Knowing

If
We've
Lived many times
Before and will do
So again

Why haven't
We rid off the
Seven sin still
Governing the mind

Sadly, our
Story is laden with
The thick layers of
Ignorance;
Instigating hatred,
Violence's and wars
Without an end

I mean,
Why haven't
We changed our
Human nature at
The core after all...

Big Game

Reality
Always in flux
As a
Consequence,

There is
The ever change
And disorder and
Humans keep
Bobbing into such
A turmoil realm

I mean,
In such a milieu,
How do we pursue
Noble mission, "To
Know the Self and the
Surrounding world,
***In toto!* "**

The Issue

Either we're
Or we're not
The awareness
In its fullest sense

I mean
Either we're
Conceptual reality
Here or keep
Wondering the world
Beyond forever

Why such
An intense curiosity
To be in action by
The three-pound
Thinking machine?

Either it is or
It is not
That's the choice
Yet to be made
And that's the
Shaky track we've
Been on for a long...

Best yet
To Come

It is love
That conquers
Beauty and goodness
Of every throbbing
Heart

It is
A creative
Thought that moves
The world at its core

It is
Moral will
That lifts humanity
To the apotheosis of
It's very best

History
Always a standing
Challenge demanding
To conquor the mind and
Asking to write new
Chapters where
" Harmony, Peace and
Rational perspective shall
Be the futuristic world of
The young everywhere..."

Daily
Prayer

I am
My possibilities
And that's
The derivation from
The inner being and
That's the
Inspiration to justify
The journey I am on

I am
Born for a purpose
Driven existence
Where
Am rolling along with
My moral courage and
Indefatigable will to win

I must be also
Aware, "What's the
Significance of my being
While am here for a brief!"

Mortal
Being

Human
What a
Spontaneity of
Creative thought

He knows
The complexity
Of the reality that's
Been on the scene
For sometimes

Let him
Face the challenge
That's been starring
Through the time

And let it be
The very essence;
Defining his strong
Will to be triumphant
All the way to the end...

On
Guard

When a
Belief
At times turn
Into a cavern of
Subjective notion

Yes, into
The drama of
Egregiousness and
Bit irrational as well

Humans often
Fall into such a pit;
Taking long time
To escape the cage

Well
The thought
Of Divine may be
Par excellence, but
His inferential entity
Warrants some rational
Reservations at times...

Awareness
Is Freedom

We're
The mystery in
This human form
Yes, we exists
Here and now, or
May be over there,
But we do exists for
Sure

Wonder,
If there's
Confirmation,
"If we're the
Omnipresence
At the same time"

We're
Explorers still
Looking for meaning,
"Who we're and what
We can become"

As we journey
From past to
Present and to future
Do we still hold the
Constant truth always!

Imposition

On scanning
The whole world
Through the time

Perhaps,
"We alone are the
Emblem of glorious
Creative thoughts
In this magnifique
Universe"

Mustn't we
Take a giant leap
And be free
From the subjective
Chain of thoughts

Let's learn to
Ask right question,
"What is our
Truth and how do we
Fit into this complexes
Scheme called, "Reality,
At last"

Legacy

Is it not
Time to rethink,
"New thoughts, new
Vision...a new direction"

I mean,
"How do we transform
Ourselves from these
Turmoil's to the tranquil
State of human experience"

If we
Can think along this
Line, why not then roll
The dice and go beyond

Let us begin
To assess,
"Where do we go
From here to define
A legacy that we all
Wishes to leave behind...

Treasure

The notion,
"Absolute"
Perhaps a mere
Illusive concept;
Oscillating in the
Mind for a long

May be
An enduring
Fantasy from
Nothingness into
Something else

It may be
A sublimal
Projection
To justify what
We ought to be

Or, it's just
An invented
Inspiration

May be
A base reference,
"What is a pure
Self-consciousness,
Sensu strictu..."

Finite
Souls

Let it
Reverberate the
Entire universe
With these hymns:

"We're born
To be the moral
Illumination and
Rational insight"

Let it
Be known by the
Entire universe,
"We're the
Finite spirits who're
On the way to
Seek our collective
Truth"

That's the
Justification of our
Noble births and
That's the reason
We must keep rolling
Toward the splendors of
Our anticipated Truth...

Fearless

Why not
Let the unity of
Virtues be the
Unstoppable force

And, be bold to
Hold the mystique of
The Truth

A Truth
That's the manifest
Perfect being to be

A Truth
Guiding the willing
Spirit to explore all
That is

A Truth
Where we're
The Totality-of-all-
Human-experience...

Humanity

At the
End of the day
Life is worth lived
If we've strengthened
Inner intention from
Self-love to the selfless
Love

That's the
Steep climb to the
Realm of Perfection,
But that's the only
Access to the truth,
We've been seeking

Only, at such
A turning point,
We emerge as one
Concrete moral reality

And with it,
We gain the awesome
Power to change the
World for good in an
Instant...

JAGDISH J. BHATT, PhD
Brings 45 years of academic experience
including a post- doctorate research scientist
at Stanford University, CA. He holds an
impressive authorship of 50 books.

Made in the USA
Columbia, SC
02 September 2022

65700622R00085